T0158820

SayWatsReal

SPEAKING, CONFESSING & APPLYING FAITH
BASED TRUTH INTO YOUR LIFE

JULIUS J. SHELBY

WESTBOW
PRESS®
A DIVISION OF THOMAS NELSON
& ZONDERVAN

WestBow Press books may be ordered through booksellers or by contacting:

WestBow Press
A Division of Thomas Nelson & Zondervan
1663 Liberty Drive
Bloomington, IN 47403
www.westbowpress.com
1 (866) 928-1240

ISBN: 978-1-9736-0094-7 (sc)

Print information available on the last page.

WestBow Press rev. date: 10/02/2017

Ephesians 4:29 New International Version (NIV)

Do not let any unwholesome talk come out of your mouths, but only what is helpful for building others up according to their needs, that it may benefit those who listen.

This Book is used as a daily devotion to uplift, inspire, motivate and build Faith in people by reading and confessing these truths and applying the word of God to their lives.

Acknowledgements

I would like to thank God for giving me the opportunity and the gift to share the word of God with his people. I am truly grateful to be called by God to inspire and impact so many peoples lives by spreading the Gospel and speaking Truth. I want to express my gratitude to all of my family, friends, and others who have supported me throughout my life. To grandma Darlene, I love and thank you so much granny. To my parents Julius & Denise Shelby, nothing that I do would be possible without you. Thank you for loving me and raising me to be the young man I am today, I love you.

I would like to thank my Senior Pastors Roosevelt & Lady LaFonda Bradley Jr. and Life Church International who serve as my spiritual parents in whom inspires me and are a key component to my spiritual growth through their actions of Faith, teachings, and prayers.

Others who I would like to express gratitude and thanks to are Rosetta Elkins-Thomas, Floyd, Kyle, Donald, and Deontae better known as "The Crew". Famous Hulbert, Alexis Wallace and late Romaine Elkins.

Last but not least this book is dedicated to my late grandfather Roosevelt Bradley Sr. and late friend, teammate and brother Demarius Reed. God calling both of you home with him not even a full two months of each other was devastating to me, but also changed my life in so many ways in which I can say God never makes mistakes even when we don't understand. I know you both cannot read this, but I live each day hoping I am making you all proud and accomplishing all the things in life we talked for days and years about. Love you PaPa and lil baby

"What is Faith? Faith is the ability to go into the unseen and bring it into the seen Quoted by Julius Shelby

Hebrews 11:1 "Faith is the substance of things hoped for, and the evidence not seen"

"Why me God? Wait Why not me?"
-Often times we doubt ourselves and think that we are not qualified or worthy for things that God has planned for us or when he assigns us to something.
God always choose the unqualified and he uses us for his Glory.

"Understand Somebody have to make an intelligent decision"
Quoted by Roosevelt Bradley Sr.

"You are the seed so whatever or whoever you let water you will determine how you grow"
Quoted by Julius Shelby

"Remember Jesus said to whom much is given much is required" think about the things you want, but also think about what it takes to get them"
Quoted by Julius Shelby

"If its not intentionally perfected it will be intentionally ignored"
Quoted by Roosevelt Bradley Jr.

Julius J. Shelby

"Understand you are a direct reflection of your prayer life"
Quoted by Julius Shelby

Luke 18:1 KJV " And he spake a parable unto them to this end, that men ought always to pray, and not to faint;"

"Love is the inconvenience of one's self for the convenience of someone else"
Quoted by Roosevelt Bradley Jr.

"Don't have a temporary excuse for a permanent outcome"
Quoted by Julius Shelby

"Don't let things around you distract you from what God said"
Quoted by Julius Shelby

"One of the most powerful tools in the world today is an Idea"
Quoted by Julius Shelby

Habukkah 2:2 KJV And the Lord answered me, and said, Write the vision, and make it plain upon tables, that he may run that readeth it.

"When you put all your focus on your priorities, you eliminate your distractions"
Quoted by Julius Shelby
"If you put God first and let him lead, guide and direct you, you will never be lost"

Proverbs 3:6 KJV In all thy ways acknowledge him, and he shall direct thy paths.

"You cannot lead others if you do not read and avail yourself to the knowledge and wisdom of God"
Quoted by Julius Shelby

"Incorrect thinking will cripple your decision making"
Quoted by Bishop I.V. Hilliard

"God has given you too much power to compromise"
Quoted by Julius Shelby

Luke 10:19 KJV Behold, I give unto you power to tread on serpents and scorpions, and over all the power of the enemy: and nothing shall by any means hurt you.

"Favor of God is like a trust Fund, he only invests in something he trust
When God gives you Favor, he trusts you enough with something"
Quoted by Julius Shelby

"Be Thankful for what you have; you'll end up having more. If you concentrate on what you don't have, you will never, ever have enough" Quoted by Oprah Winfrey
"What you are able to capture in the secret place of God, you will be able to display in public"- Quoted by Cash Luna

Psalm 91 He that dwelleth in the secret place of the most High shall abide under the shadow of the Almighty.
"If your love is based on someones performance or abilities then its not love"
Quoted by Julius Shelby

"God is challenging my Faith to believe on another Level"
Quoted by Julius Shelby

"God is always working on things while your worried about them, Let God work"
Quoted by Julius Shelby

"Whenever or wherever there is a problem, make sure you are the answer"
Quoted by Julius Shelby

"The grass ain't greener on the other side, its greener on the side you water"
Quoted by Lady LaFonda Bradley

"Remember don't let others opinion ruin the Future you see"
Quoted by Julius Shelby

"When the devil is trying to attack you with any and everything possible, attack him back with prayer, Faith, and the word of God"
Quoted by Julius Shelby

"7 Steps & Principles of protecting and maintaining your success"

1. Protect your mission from uncommitted people
2. Protect your principles from the undisciplined
3. Protect your morals from those driven by personal appetite
4. Protect the truth from the man Pleasers
5. Protect your vision from the opinions of the complacent
6. Protect your Liberty from controllers and manipulators
7. Empower your mission with proven and committed people

Quoted by Dr. Jessie Duplantis

"It is very critical to your Future that you protect your dreams from unbelievers and doubters"
Quoted by Julius Shelby

"Understand an immature mind cannot function well in a mature environment"
Quoted by Julius Shelby

"Understand there is a difference between a positive seed and negative seed, but know both of them have the ability to grow"
Quoted by Julius Shelby

"The stronger you build your spirit man, the easier you can control your flesh" Quoted by Julius Shelby

Galatians 5:16-17 KJV

This I say then, Walk in the Spirit, and ye shall not fulfill the lust of the flesh.

For the flesh lusteth against the Spirit, and the Spirit against the flesh: and these are contrary the one to the other: so that ye cannot do the things that ye would.

"Remember what you speak out of your mouth is what you have"
Quoted by Julius Shelby

Proverbs 18:21 KJV Death and life are in the power of the tongue: and they that love it shall eat the fruit thereof.

"When you feel like you have it Rock bottom, remember Jesus is the Rock at the bottom"
Quoted by Julius Shelby

"Realize you should never struggle with something you have power and authority over"
Quoted by Julius Shelby

Luke 9:1 KJV Then he called his twelve disciples together, and gave them power and authority over all devils, and to cure diseases.

"You have to hire your Faith, If your faith is unemployed, then that means your Faith is not working"
Quoted by Julius Shelby

James 2:26 KJV For as the body without the spirit is dead, so faith without works is dead also.

"*Understand changing your way of thinking, helps you change your actions*"
Quoted by Julius Shelby

"Realize God never asked you to pay for it, he asked you to Believe for it"
Quoted by Julius Shelby

Mark 11:24 KJV Therefore I say unto you, What things soever ye desire, when ye pray, believe that ye receive them, and ye shall have them.

"Remember procrastination is failure in slow motion" WHAT ARE YOU WAITING FOR!!!
Quoted by Julius Shelby

"The two most important days in your life are the day you born and the day you find out why"
Quoted by Mark Twain

"Do not cry and mourn over what God removed, when God removes something he always replaces it"
Quoted by Julius Shelby

1 Samuel 16:1 The Lord said to Samuel, "How long will you mourn for Saul, since I have rejected him as king over Israel? Fill your horn with oil and be on your way; I am sending you to Jesse of Bethlehem. I have chosen one of his sons to be king.

"Be aware of the things you let into your ear gates, especially the things of temptation" Quoted by Julius Shelby

Matthew 4:1-4 KJV Then was Jesus led up of the Spirit into the wilderness to be tempted of the devil. And when he had fasted forty days and forty nights, he was afterward an hungred. And when the tempter came to him, he said, If thou be the Son of God, command that these stones be made bread. But he answered and said, It is written, Man shall not live by bread alone, but by every word that proceedeth out of the mouth of God.

"*Your mind has to be challenged before it can be changed*"
Quoted by Julius Shelby

"If God is the creator of your destiny and purpose, why would you let anyone try and dictate your future"
Quoted by Julius Shelby

Jeremiah1:5 KJV Before I formed you in the womb I knew you, before you were born I set you apart; I appointed you as a prophet to the nations

"We FAIL because we don't OBEY GOD" Quoted by Julius Shelby

Deuteronomy 28:15 KJV However, if you do not obey the Lord your God and do not carefully follow all his commands and decrees I am giving you today, all these curses will come on you and overtake you:

"Changing the date on the calendar is not as important as how you live the day"
Quoted by Julius Shelby

"You cannot run the race that God has called you to run if you are out of shape"
Quoted by Julius Shelby

"Understand mans opinion and thoughts doesn't rule over Gods plan"
Quoted by Julius Shelby

Jeremiah 29:11 KJV For I know the thoughts that I think toward you, saith the Lord, thoughts of peace, and not of evil, to give you an expected end.

"Hearing Gods voice is key, but your response is connected to Gods release" Quoted by Julius Shelby

Genesis 12:1-5 KJV Now the Lord had said unto Abram, Get thee out of thy country, and from thy kindred, and from thy father's house, unto a land that I will shew thee: And I will make of thee a great nation, and I will bless thee, and make thy name great; and thou shalt be a blessing: And I will bless them that bless thee, and curse him that curseth thee: and in thee shall all families of the earth be blessed. So Abram departed, as the Lord had spoken unto him; and Lot went with him: and Abram was seventy and five years old when he departed out of Haran. And Abram took Sarai his wife, and Lot his brother's son, and all their substance that they had gathered, and the souls that they had gotten in Haran; and they went forth to go into the land of Canaan; and into the land of Canaan they came.

"Don't look for God to bless you, if you cannot bless him with Praises"
Quoted by Julius Shelby

Psalm 34:1KJV I will bless the Lord at all times: his praise shall continually be in my mouth.

Julius J. Shelby

"There should be two daily requirements we as people should have, Thank God an be a Blessing to someone"
Quoted by Julius Shelby

"Always remember the Lord is mindful of you" When is he mindful of you? ALL THE TIME!!!
Quoted by Julius Shelby

Psalms 115:12 KJV The Lord hath been mindful of us: he will bless us; he will bless the house of Israel; he will bless the house of Aaron.

"Understand you should not wast time fighting things or people that are not in your weight class"
Quoted by Julius Shelby

"The level you serve God on, is the level you Love God on"
Quoted by Julius Shelby

"Understand every Blessing will always be traced back to a seed; Track you seed"
Quoted by Julius Shelby

"Realize the enemy always wants to isolate you when your on the edge of a breakthrough"
Quoted by Julius Shelby

"Remember Life is not about hiding and waiting for the storm to pass but learning how to command the storm to stop"
Quoted by Julius Shelby

Mark 4:39 KJV And he arose, and rebuked the wind, and said unto the sea, Peace, be still. And the wind ceased, and there was a great calm.

"*Understand you are the Kingdom display that showcase God before all men; They must see the God in you*"
Quoted by Julius Shelby

Matthew 5:16 KJV Let your light so shine before men, that they may see your good works, and glorify your Father which is in heaven.

"Remember you are made in the Image of God, Know who you are"
Quoted by Julius Shelby

Genesis 1:27 KJV So God created man in his own image, in the image of God created he him; male and female created he them.

"Understand God will put you in places for development, and not for permanent dwelling"
Quoted by Julius Shelby

"Don't trade away Gods lifelong gift for you in order to satisfy a short term pleasure; never trade away your blessing from God for carnal gratification from the Devil"
Quoted by Julius Shelby

"Remember your gift will get you to the place, but your character will keep you there"
Quoted by Julius Shelby

Proverbs 18:16 KJV A man's gift maketh room for him, and bringeth him before great men.

""*The sin of this world has spoke her mind, when will the church speak hers?*"
Quoted by Julius Shelby

"*Don't be afraid of the decline because one day you will have to take credit for the success*"
Quoted by Craig Groschel

"*Understand Faith is your spiritual Wifi in which you cannot see, but you can connect to it whenever you need it*"
Quoted by Julius Shelby

"*Understand prayer is a divine spiritual communication between you and God in which prepares you for the supernatural manifestation of God*"
Quoted by Julius Shelby

"You cannot try and change your environment until you change yourself"
Quoted by Julius Shelby

"Remember when you're anointed you will always be in a place where there is a need, God uses anointed people"
Quoted by Julius Shelby

"Stop asking God to make your burdens light, but instead ask him to make you stronger to overcome them"
Quoted by Julius Shelby

"Stop focusing on all the things that are not working, Focus on the one thing that will work"
Quoted by Julius Shelby

"Things will work out better for you if you pray more and say less" Pray & be Quiet; Try it it works!"
Quoted by Julius Shelby

"Don't think of the things you didn't receive after praying. Think of the countless blessings God gave you without even asking him"
Quoted by Julius Shelby

"Understand spiritual maturity isn't measured by how well you can quote the bible or jump in shout, but how straight you can walk in obedience to Gods word"
Quoted by Julius Shelby

"Realize the enemy is not after your money or materialistic things. He wants your mind, your will, your heart, your peace, your Faith. You are not being attacked over the tangible things in your life, the enemy is fighting you over the things that are not seen"
Quoted by Julius Shelby

"Never interrupt your enemy why he's making a mistake"
Quoted by Napoleon

"When you cant control what's happening, challenge yourself to control the way you respond to what's happening. That's where your Power is!"
Quoted by Julius Shelby

"If you can't take your own advice, don't give it to anyone else to take, it may be good advice but is it the right advice?"
Quoted by Julius Shelby

"The more anger you carry in your heart towards the past, the less capable you are of loving in the present." LET IT GO!
Quoted by Julius Shelby

"Lord, when we long for life without difficulties, remind us that oaks grow strong in contrary winds and diamonds are made under pressure."
Quoted by Peter Marshall

"When one door closes, another opens; but we often look so long and so regretfully upon closed doors that we do not see the one which has opened for us"
Quoted by Alexander Graham Bell

"Watch the things you say out of anger because the anger will fade away, but the words will linger around"
Quoted by Julius Shelby

"Don't allow the enemy to try and deceive you about you"
Quoted by Julius Shelby

"What God expects out of you is already in you, its just up to you to tap into it and bring it out"
Quoted by Julius Shelby

"Understand God puts you in situations that only Faith can get you out of"
Quoted by Julius Shelby

Confessions

"I will live my life happy" Quoted by Julius Shelby

"I will love God with all my heart" Quoted by Julius Shelby

"I will mature and grow daily in every area of my life" Quoted by Julius Shelby

"I will show and express love daily" Quoted by Julius Shelby

"I will keep God first" Quoted by Julius Shelby

"I believe God and I have the Faith to have everything God has in store for me"
Quoted by Julius Shelby

"God is my source and he supplies me with resources to get what I need"
Quoted by Julius Shelby

"I am healed and have been made whole in Jesus name" Quoted by Julius Shelby

"I believe God, I believe his word" Quoted by Julius Shelby

"I am the righteousness of God" Quoted by Julius Shelby

"I commit to live a healthy lifestyle this day" Quoted by Julius Shelby

"I walk by Faith and not by sight" Quoted by Julius Shelby

"I have whatever I say in Jesus name" Quoted by Julius Shelby

"My life shall be filled with Gods supernatural favor in Jesus name"
Quoted by Julius Shelby

"I live under the direction of the holy spirit"
Quoted by Julius Shelby

"I decree and declare I am blessed in Jesus name"
Quoted by Julius Shelby

"I decree and declare my family and friends are blessed in Jesus name"
Quoted by Julius Shelby

"I walk in full authority that God has given me in Jesus name"
Quoted by Julius Shelby

"This day shall be a great and prosperous day in Jesus name"
Quoted by Julius Shelby

"This day I will defeat the enemy by Faith against any of his attacks"
Quoted by Julius Shelby

"I will Trust God with everything in my Life"
Quoted by Julius Shelby

"I will live my life by the Word of God" Quoted by Julius Shelby

"I will not allow my past to ruin my future"
Quoted by Julius Shelby

"I will not let fear control my decisions" Quoted by Julius Shelby

"I am a cheerful and generous giver" Quoted by Julius Shelby

"I will not complain, instead I will be grateful" Quoted by Julius Shelby

"My words are powerful, therefore I will speak with purpose"
Quoted by Julius Shelby

"Nothing is impossible because I believe God"
Quoted by Julius Shelby

"I will not let pride set in my heart" Quoted by Julius Shelby

"My thoughts will line up with Gods will" Quoted by Julius Shelby

"I grow from Faith to Faith" Quoted by Julius Shelby

"I will use the power God has given me" Quoted by Julius Shelby

"My flesh has no control over me" Quoted by Julius Shelby

"I can forgive those who have hurt me" Quoted by Julius Shelby

"I can forgive and love my enemies" Quoted by Julius Shelby

"I will serve God with my whole heart" Quoted by Julius Shelby

"I will walk in the supernatural favor of God" Quoted by Julius Shelby

"I will walk in the supernatural power of God" Quoted by Julius Shelby

"I decree and declare I will not live in poverty" Quoted by Julius Shelby

"I decree and declare all curses are broken over my life" Quoted by Julius Shelby

"I bring light to a dark place" Quoted by Julius Shelby

The seeds I sow will grow and manifest in Jesus name" Quoted by Julius Shelby

"I am no longer a prisoner of my past" Quoted by Julius Shelby

I am stronger than I was yesterday" Quoted by Julius Shelby

"I will fulfill the purpose God has for me" Quoted by Julius Shelby

"I am above and not beneath" Quoted by Julius Shelby

'I pray today will be the best day of my life" Quoted by Julius Shelby

"All debt in my life is cancelled in Jesus name" Quoted by Julius Shelby

"Today I will be a blessing to someone else" Quoted by Julius Shelby

"I will not be ashamed to tell the world about Jesus Christ" Quoted by Julius Shelby

Connect with Julius!

Facebook: www.facebook.com/julius.shelby.9

Instagram: instagram.com/heartmy__pics

Twitter: www.twitter.com/Ambition_15

Email: julius5shelby@yahoo.com

Website: http://www.saywatsreal.bigcartel.com